SURVIVAL GUIDE
TO PETS

Written and illustrated by
Scoular Anderson

Also available in Lions

Survival Guide to Parents
by Scoular Anderson

Survival Guide to School
Survival Guide to Friends
by Brough Girling

Survival Guide to Pets was first published in
Great Britain in Lions in 1995

1 3 5 7 9 10 8 6 4 2

Lions is an imprint of HarperCollins Children's Books,
a division of HarperCollins Publishers Ltd, 77–85 Fulham
Palace Road, Hammersmith, London W6 8JB

Copyright © Scoular Anderson 1995

The author asserts the moral right to be identified
as the author of the work.

Printed and bound in Great Britain
by HarperCollins Manufacturing Ltd, Glasgow

0 00 675015 X

CONTENTS

1 What are Pets?   5
2 Why do People have Pets?   10
3 Dogs   14
4 Cats   33
5 Tortoises   48
6 Goldfish   52
7 Small Furry Things   54
8 Budgies   58
9 Elephants   64
10 Unusual Cats   68
11 Sloths   72
12 Wildebeest or Gnus   73
13 Hyenas   76
14 Snakes   77
15 Unusual Birds   82
16 Creepy-Crawlies   86

WHAT ARE PETS?

Pets are animals which are owned by human beings. As they live in the humans' houses they are not usually very big. The animals have to be trained to live sensibly in houses. Some of them might even understand a few words of human speech. COMPET, our voice-activated computer, will give you the correct scientific name. Show, COMPET!

COMPET will give you an example of the type of animal we are talking about. Type, COMPET!

Here are some examples of the most common Personal Easily-Trained Species. Types, COMPET!

Look at them closely. Do you have anything that resembles any of these? If you do, you have P.E.T.S.

If you are still not sure if you have P.E.T.S., use this flow-chart to identify any strange creatures in your house.

START HERE

IS THE CREATURE COMPLETELY COVERED IN HAIR?

DOES IT MAKE THIS NOISE? "WOOF-WOOF" OR "YOWL!"

YES — YOU HAVE A DOG OR EVEN A WOLF.

NO — DOES IT MAKE THIS NOISE? "MIAOW, MIAOW.

DOES IT HAVE HAIR JUST HERE AND THERE?

YES — THIS IS A HUMAN BEING. PROBABLY A MEMBER OF YOUR FAMILY.

NO — OR IT COULD BE A PETS WITH A BAD SKIN CONDITION. PETS LIKE THIS NEED VETS.

DOES IT HAVE FEATHERS AND A HOOKED BEAK?

NO — DOES IT LIVE UNDER WATER?

YES — ARE THE FEATHERS BLUE?

NO — YOU HAVE AN EAGLE OR A VULTURE. KEEP ALL OTHER SMALL PETS IN A SEPARATE ROOM.

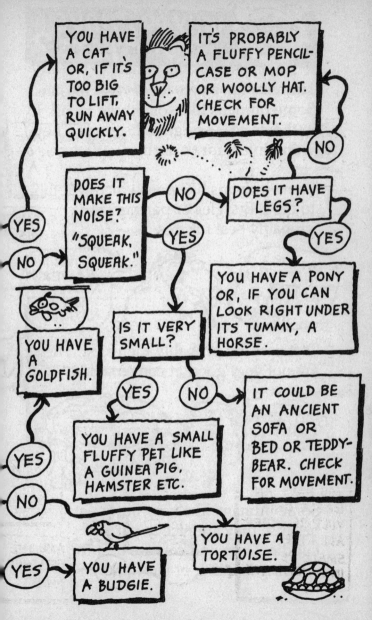

9

WHY DO PEOPLE HAVE PETS?

CHAPTER 2

Humans have pets for several reasons. Some humans like something to talk to and pets are very good listeners. They won't interrupt or argue.

Some humans like pets which will talk to *them*. Budgies or parrots are probably best for this.

Tortoises are probably the worst. They are not very good at conversation.

Some humans like very fluffy pets because they are nice to pat and cuddle. Dogs and cats are best for stroking, tickling or cuddling.

Some humans like to brush or wash their pets. Dogs and ponies are tops for this sort of thing.

Tortoises are at the bottom of the cuddly league. They're not very fluffy so brushing is out. You could dust them now and then.

Some humans like pets which are very active. Some like to be active with their pet, e.g. walking the dog or riding a horse. Others just like to watch small furry pets scurrying about.

Don't get a tortoise if you like to watch scurrying. If you take a tortoise for a walk in the park you'll be away for a fortnight.

So, if you haven't already got pets, think carefully before you buy one. We're going to look at pets in more detail – and how to survive them. However . . .
WARNING!!
You will never survive pets if *you* are not in control. Pets have to know just who is the boss.
This means YOU.

However, pets want to be the boss too. If you lose control and let them be the boss you will never survive pets.
You will become PETrified.

Here is an example of petrification.

Here is an example of even worse petrification.

GRRRR! SNARL!!

CHAPTER 3 — DOGS

Dogs come in a huge range of shapes, sizes, colours, coats* etc. Here is a selection:

*This is short for PETticoat. Most pets wear these. They are warm, waterproof, furry garments which don't have buttons or zips.

Here are the main things you should
beware of in a dog. Show Dogfax,
COMPET!

* HUGE AMOUNTS OF ENERGY
* FOND OF PRACTICAL JOKES
* BOTTOMLESS PIT FOR A STOMACH
* SHAGGY, DAMP AND SMELLY
* CRAFTY
* VERY EMOTIONAL
* IDENTITY CRISIS

COMPET

Let's look at the last point first –
'Identity Crisis'. This needs a little
explaining . . .

Compare these two scenes from family life:

One scene is the human view, the other is the dog's view.

The problem with dogs is, they think they're human (or they think humans are dogs). This leads to trouble.
For instance, dogs think they can sit where humans sit.

Dogs think they can sleep in human beds and eat human food.

There is very little you can do about this. You could try to learn dog-speak (A very difficult language for humans to get their tongues round) then explain the problem to your pet.

*LISTEN, CLOTH EARS, SIT ON MY BED JUST ONE MORE TIME AND YOU'LL BE KIPPING IN THE GARAGE FOR EVER MORE!

WHUMP!
THUMP!
RIP!
WE APOLOGIZE FOR THE INTERFERENCE.
SOME PETS ARE LOOSE IN THIS BOOK.
THEY WILL BE ROUNDED UP AS SOON AS POSSIBLE.
COMPET!

Let's turn to the other dog characteristics:

✳ HUGE AMOUNTS OF ENERGY

Dogs would go 'Walkies' every minute of the day if they got the chance. Compare these two 'Walkies' patterns. Patterns, COMPET!

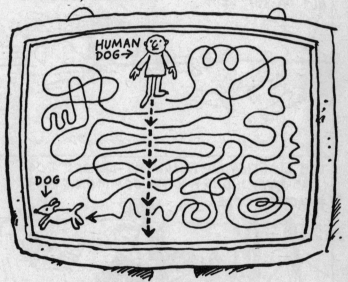

A dog will 'Walkies' a trillion times the distance of a humandog. It's a good idea to try and tire a dog out so it won't bother you later but BEWARE! . . .

The aim of the dog is to tire out the humandog. Here are some things you should look out for. They are known as:

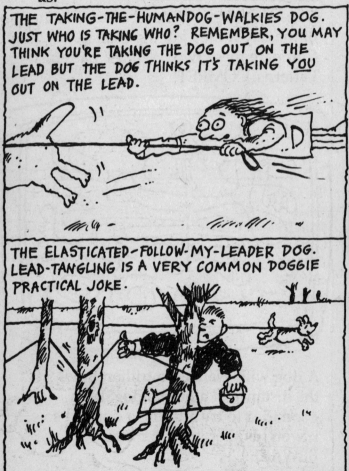

THE TAKING-THE-HUMANDOG-WALKIES DOG. JUST WHO IS TAKING WHO? REMEMBER, YOU MAY THINK YOU'RE TAKING THE DOG OUT ON THE LEAD BUT THE DOG THINKS IT'S TAKING <u>YOU</u> OUT ON THE LEAD.

THE ELASTICATED-FOLLOW-MY-LEADER DOG. LEAD-TANGLING IS A VERY COMMON DOGGIE PRACTICAL JOKE.

THE JUST-ONE-MORE-THROW DOG.
A DOG WILL CHASE A BALL/STICK FOR EVER
AND EVER. IT WILL BRING IT BACK FOR EVER
AND EVER, TOO. THIS LEAVES THE DOG PANTING
WITH EXCITEMENT AND THE HUMANDOG
PANTING WITH EXHAUSTION.

HARDLY ENOUGH ENERGY TO THROW FOR THE 543 RD TIME

THE WILD-COUNTRYSIDE-WALKIE-DOGGIE.
SOME DOGS GO COMPLETELY OVER THE TOP AND
RUN THROUGH DITCHES, BRAMBLES, THICKETS,
CANALS, BRACKEN, BOGS, DRAINS, SEWAGE-PIPES,
COW-PATS, ETC., ETC. THE HUMANDOG THEN
HAS TO SPEND HOURS CLEANING THE DOG UP.
THIS IS ANOTHER DOGGIE PRACTICAL JOKE.

✳ BOTTOMLESS PIT AS A STOMACH

All this fooling around makes a dog constantly hungry. This has advantages and disadvantages.

SMALL DOGS CAN BE USED AS VACUUM-CLEANERS TO CLEAN UP CRUMBS

BUT SOME DOGS BELIEVE THEY CAN SUCK FOOD OFF PLATES WITH THEIR EYES. KEEP LARGE DOGS LIKE THIS AWAY FROM NERVOUS GUESTS

As humandog food is much more interesting than dog food, a dog can't understand why *it* gets brown, gooey stuff out of a tin rather than roast chicken, chips, iced buns, hamburgers etc.

Try to make your dog's menu as interesting as possible.

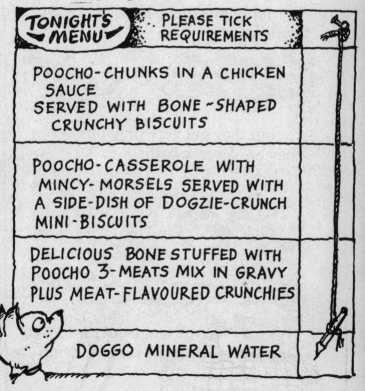

TONIGHT'S MENU | PLEASE TICK REQUIREMENTS

POOCHO-CHUNKS IN A CHICKEN SAUCE
SERVED WITH BONE-SHAPED CRUNCHY BISCUITS

POOCHO-CASSEROLE WITH MINCY-MORSELS SERVED WITH A SIDE-DISH OF DOGZIE-CRUNCH MINI-BISCUITS

DELICIOUS BONE STUFFED WITH POOCHO 3-MEATS MIX IN GRAVY PLUS MEAT-FLAVOURED CRUNCHIES

DOGGO MINERAL WATER

You will find that dogs happily run about in the rain . . .

. . . submerge themselves in muddy puddles . . .

. . . but they get very unhappy when they are given a bath.

This may seem strange but the fact is, dogs were born to be shaggy, damp and smelly.

Some people like to have their dogs regularly groomed and clipped. Think before you try this. If your dog has been shaggy for a long time, you may be in for a nasty surprise.

UNCLIPPED

CLIPPED

It's a great mistake to try and make a dog tidy and sweet-smelling. It will just go and make itself even untidier and smellier than before.

The best plan is to wear nose plugs or cover your dog's coat with a dog-coat.

...ery crafty. They are always ...o outwit their owners. Be on ...guard at all times.

...ere are a couple of common doggie crafty tricks:

IF A DOG THINKS YOU'RE GOING OUT, IT WILL PRETEND TO BE A DOORMAT AT THE FRONT DOOR, READY TO LEAP OUT AS SOON AS THE DOOR IS OPENED.

YAWNING, LOOKING UP AT THE SKY,
HUMMING QUIETLY TO ITSELF — THESE ARE
ALL CRAFTY RUSES A DOG USES TO HIDE
THE FACT THAT IT HAS JUST EATEN A WHOLE
PACKET OF CHOCOLATE BISCUITS IT DISCOVERED
IN A SHOPPING-BAG ON THE KITCHEN FLOOR

Lastly, DO NOT BE FOOLED by dogs acting in an emotional way. A dog will put on an Oscar-winning performance if everyone decides to go out and leave it at home.

A dog will be perfectly happy in the house by itself.

RUMBLE!
RUMBLE!
WATCH OUT! LOOSE PETS ON THE RUN! CLOSE THIS BOOK UNTIL THEY PASS!

RUMBLE!

ALL CLEAR!

CHAPTER 4

CATS

Cats don't come in as many shapes and sizes as dogs. There is one basic model and a few variations. Cats, COMPET!

THE CAT →

THE HAIRY CAT ↓

THE NOT SO HAIRY CAT ↓

THE STRIPY CAT →

COMPET

Here are the main things you should watch out for in cats if you want to survive them. Show Catfax, COMPET!

* STRANGE SENSE OF HUMOUR
* OPERA-LOVING
* CUSHION COMPLEX
* BEING SUPERIOR
* BEING FAMOUS
* CLAWS

Cats have a very strange sense of
humour. The most famous cat joke is
one that humans fall for every time –
the cat in the tree joke: a cat climbs up
a tree and pretends it can't get down.

Humans then have to get ladders – or
even call the fire brigade to bring
ladders – to get the cat down.
Cats will meet up with their pals after
these joke sessions and roll about
helpless with laughter.

Cats love opera – especially in the middle of the night. The trouble is, their idea of singing is different from ours. Here is a short video of a cat opera. It will help you enjoy cat music. Subtitles are provided.

36

*I LOVE YOUR DAINTY PAWS AND YOUR SHINING WHISKERS! OH, CARMEN ARE YOU THERE?

*PUSH OFF, FLEABAG! I WAIT FOR ANOTHER! HARK, HERE HE COMES!

*WHAT'S THIS? A SCOUNDREL UNDER MY BELOVED CARMEN'S BALCONY!

38

✳ CUSHION COMPLEX

While dogs are busy rushing about all day, cats prefer to sit around on cushions or pretend to be cushions. You can find cats being cushions almost anywhere. Examples, COMPET.

COMPET

40

Even worse, cats often treat humans as cushions. Show, COMPET.

This is because cats think they are superior to humans. (See next page.)

✳ BEING SUPERIOR

Cats feel they are superior to human beings. This is how they see themselves in the animal kingdom. Kingdom, COMPET!

LEVEL 1   CATS

LEVEL 2   ELEPHANTS, WOMBATS ETC.

LEVEL 3   HUMANS

LEVEL 4   WRIGGLY THINGS

LEVEL 5   WET THINGS

LEVEL 6   DOGS

COMPET

Cats remain aloof from ghastly human habits like slurping their tea, snoring, picking their noses etc. You will nearly always see a cat with a look of superiority on its face.

Always be on your best behaviour in front of a cat and mind your manners. When a cat stops being superior and becomes friendly and gets very close – e.g. rubbing itself against your legs –

BEWARE! It's only doing this in the hope that its fleas will jump onto your legs.

✷ BEING FAMOUS

Cats feel they are superior to other creatures because they have had lots of things named after them. This makes them think they're famous. Cat fame, COMPET!

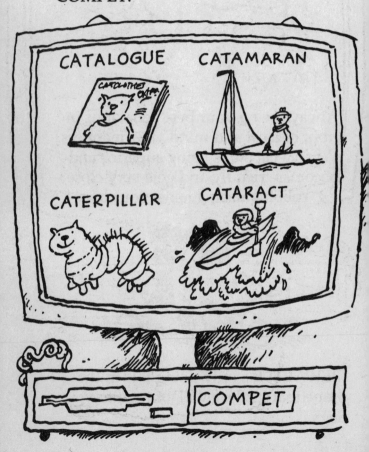

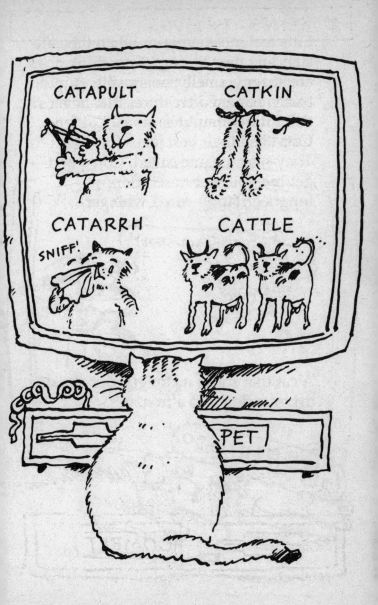

Cats feel most superior when they are standing next to dogs. Cats think dogs are shaggy, smelly, noisy, silly, stupid, badly-designed creatures that never sit still for two minutes.

Cats keep their best jokes for dogs. They play a game called 'Come-and-get-me-you-wet-nosed-floppy-tongued-flappy-eared-whinger'.

A cat that sticks its tongue out at a dog drives a dog into a frenzy.

The cat keeps just out of reach until the dog is a frothy, yapping ball of fur. Then the cat produces . . .

...CLAWS

EEEEEOOo!

NEVER get between a cat and a dog during a joke session!
(See also section on unusual cats)

Now let's look at some other pets. Tortoises don't chase after sticks or climb trees. They're so quiet you might forget that they're there – in fact, they can be a bit boring . . .

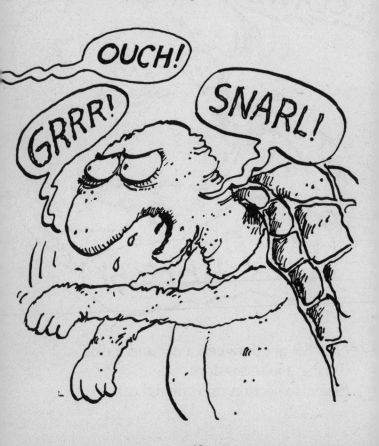

Let's begin again . . .
Tortoises are incredibly clever. They
are very energetic and like all types of
sport. They are very quiet and well-
behaved. They don't bite or scratch,
bark or howl. They won't cost you a
fortune in tinned food or biscuits or
rubber toys.
Tortoises are not boring in the
slightest. Several tortoises have written
books and a French tortoise once
climbed to the top of Mount Everest.

In fact, tortoises are the most
wonderful pets to own and you'll have
no trouble surviving them.

CHAPTER 6 GOLDFISH

Goldfish are very houseproud. To keep them happy you must provide the following. Fishfax, COMPET!

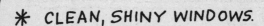

* CLEAN, SHINY WINDOWS.

* NICELY PATTERNED CARPET OF GRAVEL.

* SEVERAL HOUSEPLANTS OF THE LONG, WEEDY KIND.

* ORNAMENTS: E.G. SUNKEN SHIPS, MERMAIDS, CAVES, UNDERWATER CASTLES ETC.

COMPET

The goldfish will then swim round and round their home checking everything is in place and everything is clean.

Goldfish are very thoughtful creatures. They spend a lot of time thinking very hard. However, since they don't speak, you never learn what wonderful thoughts they're thinking.

Try not to let all this thinking get you down. Some goldfish owners have gone completely mad thinking about the thoughts their goldfish is thinking.

CHAPTER 7

SMALL FURRY THINGS

Some people prefer to have small furry things. They like them because they are confined to cages and don't roam around the house. (Although sometimes they escape from their cages and become F.U.R.R.T.I.V.E. – Forever Under Rugs, Radiators, Televisions, In Vases Etc.)

One small furry thing looks much like another small furry thing. Furry, COMPET!

But there are differences between the small furry things. They have strange names like:

Hamsters, Herbals, Gerbils, Herberts, Rarebits, Robbots, Ratbites, Rare Mice, Skinny Pigs etc.

They can be divided into four groups.

THE HARDLY-EVER-SEEN FURRY THING

THESE CREATURES STAY BURIED NEARLY ALL THE TIME IN THE SAWDUST/STRAW AT THE BACK OF THEIR CAGES.

SURVIVAL GUIDE

YOU'LL JUST HAVE TO <u>IMAGINE</u> YOU HAVE A RARE AND STRANGE-LOOKING PET. (BUT IS THE PET ACTUALLY THERE? SEE NEXT PAGE.)

THE GREAT-ESCAPING FURRY THING

SOME FURRY THINGS WILL EAT ALMOST ANYTHING, INCLUDING PARTS OF THEIR CAGE.

SURVIVAL GUIDE
IF YOUR FURRY THING AND ITS CAGE KEEP DISAPPEARING TRY A METAL CAGE SUSPENDED OVER A BATH FULL OF WATER.

THE PERPETUAL-MOTION FURRY THING

FURRY THINGS CAN BE VERY ACTIVE AND BEHAVE AS IF THEY ARE TRAINING FOR THE OLYMPICS.

SURVIVAL GUIDE
IF THIS GETS YOU DOWN, TIE VERY HEAVY GOLD MEDALS ROUND THEIR NECKS AND TELL THEM TO RELAX FOR FOUR YEARS.

THE MULTIPLYING FURRY THING

IF YOU OWN TWO OR THREE FURRY THINGS YOU MIGHT FIND YOU HAVE TWO OR THREE HUNDRED FURRY THINGS WITHIN A MONTH.

SURVIVAL GUIDE LEAVE HOME.

WARNING! More cat jokes!
Don't let a cat near a small furry thing
or the cat will try another of its
hilarious jokes.

BURP!

CHAPTER 8 BUDGIES

If you want to survive a budgie you must look out for the following things: Budgies, COMPET!

* VERY MESSY EATING HABITS.
* VERY CONCEITED.
* BORING MUSICAL TASTE.
* TALKING NON-STOP TO THEMSELVES.
* TALKING NON-STOP TO EVERYONE ELSE

COMPET

Budgies have no table-manners. They bury their heads in their feeding dishes then, when they've eaten the seeds, they throw the empty seed-cases on the floor.

Teach your budgie good manners. Try to get it to use a knife and fork and a napkin.

Budgies are very conceited. They will spend hours looking at themselves in their mirror. Sticking a picture of a vulture on the mirror might cure the habit.

AARGH! I'VE SUDDENLY BECOME UGLY!

A budgie's idea of music is to bang a little bell. This gets very boring. Try to improve your budgie's musical taste by giving it new instruments. They are not very bright so do this in two simple stages.

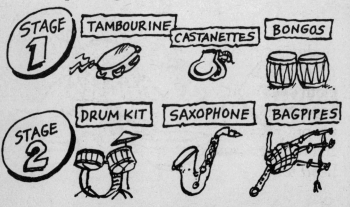

STAGE 1

TAMBOURINE   CASTANETTES   BONGOS

STAGE 2

DRUM KIT   SAXOPHONE   BAGPIPES

The most difficult thing to survive is budgie-talk. They will talk for hours and it's not even interesting talk. Here is a translation of a piece of budgie-talk:

CHIP... CHIP... TWIT... MUTTER... SQUOOK... CHIPPERCHAT...CHUP... TWITTER... TWITTER... TWOOCH... CHURP... SQUAWK... CHIRRUP... *

* SO I SAID TO COUSIN MABEL, THAT'S THE COUSIN WHOSE FATHER HAS A WOODEN LEG, I SAID. HAVE YOU TRIED THAT NEW CARPET SHAMPOO...

Budgies go quiet if you put a cloth over their cage. You could try putting a big hat over the budgie's head too.

And now we've managed to round up some of the more unusual pests ... er ... pets. If any of these frighten you, just keep still and hold the book at arm's length.

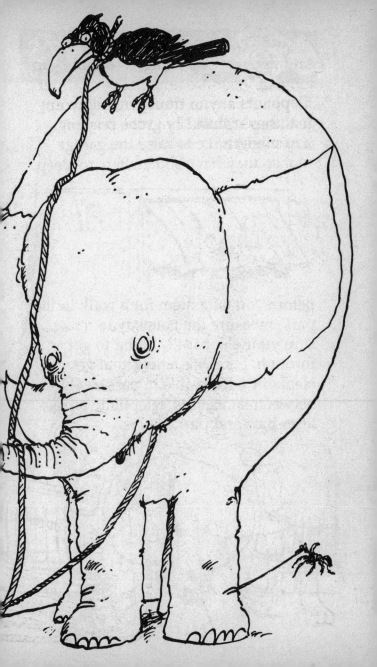

Elephants are no trouble at all except that they eventually grow very big. You might have to raise the garage roof so they have somewhere to sleep.

Before you take them for a walk in the park, measure the gateway to make sure your elephant is going to get through. Likewise, check that your elephant will be able to pass easily between lampposts, telephone boxes, litter bins and parked cars.

Don't encourage elephants to run after sticks or balls in the park. They will leave great dents in the grass and knock over trees and shrubs.

Elephants have a tremendous sense of humour. They love hearing jokes about themselves. Try telling some of these to your elephant.

Why do elephants wear green felt hats?
So they can walk across billiard tables without being seen.

Why do elephants have wrinkly ankles?
Because their shoes are too tight.

How do elephants talk to their friends?
On elephones.

What's big, grey and bounces?
An elephant on a pogo stick.

What's big, grey and scary?
An Elephantom.

What's the difference between an
elephant and a banana?
Have you ever tried to peel an elephant.

What's grey and wrinkly and has two
wheels?
An elephant on a motorbike.

How do you know if an elephant has
been in your fridge?
Footprints in the butter.

Why do elephants have trunks?
Because they'd look silly with handbags.

CHAPTER 10 — UNUSUAL CATS

A large number of people become cat-owners by adopting a stray kitten which comes to their back door. This can be a bit dodgy. Look at these photos of Kevin Trimble who found a young, lost cat in the garage. The photos were taken over several months.

You may find you have taken on
something larger than you can
manage. Small kittens can sometimes
grow into very big cats. You may end
up with a lion, tiger or puma sleeping
in the basket in the kitchen.

However, there's no reason why you
can't survive a large cat. The only
trouble you're likely to get is from
neighbours. Look out for the following
trouble-spots in neighbours' gardens.

Sloths are ideal pets for lazy people. If
you don't want an energetic watch-dog
then a watch-sloth is for you. It will
hang upside down from the curtain
rail all day and keep an eye on things.

Sloths have a habit of falling on your
head suddenly. Never stand under a
sloth. However, you may be able to
train your sloth to stun burglars by
falling on them.

Wildebeest or gnus, as they are sometimes called, are not pretty animals.

They are easy pets though.
They don't need to be taken for walks or fed from tins. All they need is a brisk brushing once a week.
The good news about wildebeest is that they eat grass. You can throw away the lawnmower and keep a wildebeest tethered on the lawn.
The bad news about wildebeest is that they are very friendly and have huge numbers of relatives. A wildebeest's relatives and friends will visit regularly . . .

BE WARNED!

Hyenas are very like wildebeest because:
(a) They're handy
(b) They have lots of friends.

Hyenas are handy because they'll eat just about anything so they're great for getting rid of rubbish – bones, potato peelings, newspapers, socks etc.

Unfortunately, they like telling really silly stories. They have all their friends round – usually after dark – and tell them silly stories. Then they all laugh in a loud, silly way.

If you're going to keep hyenas, every now and then tell them some sad facts – like how *ugly* they are. This helps to dampen silly giggling.

Snakes only eat about once a fortnight so they're very economical. They look very decorative draped round your furniture.

If you want to survive a snake be very careful which kind you get. Snakes fall into four groups. Snakes, COMPET!

THE SQUEEZING SNAKE

THE HYPNOTIZING SNAKE

THE LEAPING SNAKE

THE WEEDY SNAKE

GOOD SNAKE GUIDE

THE WEEDY SNAKE

GOOD POINTS: YOU CAN DO JUST ABOUT ANYTHING WITH A WEEDY SNAKE. HANDY STAND-IN FOR STRING/ROPE ETC.

BAD POINTS: WEEDY SNAKES DON'T HAVE A VERY GOOD IMAGE — NOT VERY MACHO. YOU MIGHT AS WELL HAVE AN EARTHWORM.

THE SQUEEZING SNAKE

GOOD POINTS: VERY AFFECTIONATE, LOVES HUGGING PEOPLE.

BAD POINTS: OVERDOES THE HUGGING SOMETIMES. DON'T LET IT HUG MORE THAN ONE ARM AT A TIME.

THE HYPNOTIZING SNAKE

GOOD POINTS: WILL SOLVE THE PROBLEM OF NAGGING PARENTS OR TALKATIVE GRANNIES BY SENDING THEM INTO A TRANCE.

BAD POINTS: DON'T LOOK INTO THE SNAKE'S EYES. ON THE OTHER HAND, KEEP AN EYE ON IT AND WEAR DARK GLASSES WHEN HANDLING.

THE LEAPING SNAKE

GOOD POINTS: WILL LEAP ON BURGLARS, STRAY CATS AND PEOPLE WHO RING YOUR DOORBELL TO ASK SILLY QUESTIONS.

BAD POINTS: WILL LEAP FROM THE TOPS OF WARDROBES OR OUT FROM UNDER TABLES AND WRAP ITS COILS ROUND YOUR LEGS. THIS IS POSSIBLY A KIND OF SNAKISH JOKE.

LEARN SNAKE SAFETY! — PLAY THE SNAKE
GAME. GET FROM START TO FINISH BY TRAVELLING
ALONG THE WEEDY SNAKES. TRY TO LOSE AS
FEW POINTS AS POSSIBLE. YOU START WITH

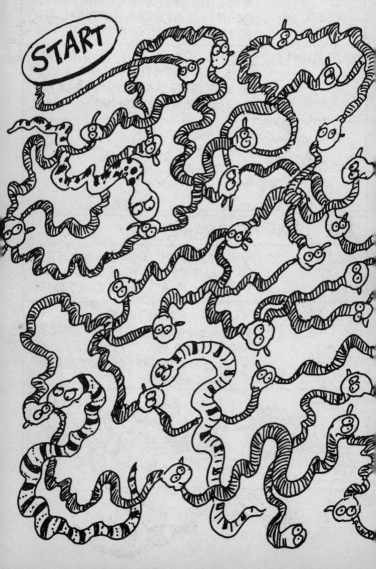

TEN POINTS BUT LOSE POINTS EVERY TIME
YOU COME FACE TO FACE WITH ANOTHER SNAKE,
IKE THIS: SQUEEZING SNAKE— LOSE 5 POINTS,
IYPNOTIZING SNAKE—3 POINTS, LEAPING SNAKE—2 POINTS.

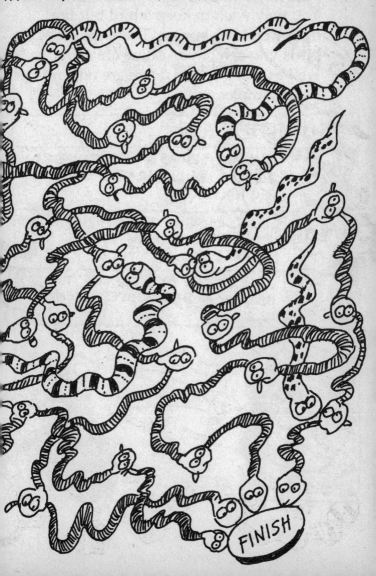

FINISH

You may wish to keep a bird but find budgies rather boring. There are other birds you can have – some are exotic as well as being useful. Here are one or two examples:

THE TOUCAN

GOOD POINTS	CAN BE USED AS A NUTCRACKER, VICE OR CONTAINER – E.G: CLOTHES-PEG HOLDER.
BAD POINTS	LIKES CRACKING OTHER THINGS BESIDES NUTS – E.G. LIGHTBULBS, RADIOS, FINGERS ETC.
SURVIVE	…THE TOUCAN BY KEEPING ITS BEAK IN A BEAK-COVER WHEN NOT IN USE.

THE OSTRICH

GOOD POINTS: CAN BE USED AS TRANSPORT TO AND FROM SCHOOL.

BAD POINTS: INCREDIBLY NOSY. ITS LONG NECK ALLOWS IT TO PEER INTO UPSTAIRS WINDOWS, UNDER BEDS AND OVER SHOWER CURTAINS.

SURVIVE ...THE OSTRICH BY MAKING IT A 'NOSYBOX'. THIS IS A COLLECTION OF COMPARTMENTS WITH PHOTOS INSIDE. THE OSTRICH CAN PEER INTO THESE TO ITS HEART'S CONTENT. CHANGE THE PHOTOS REGULARLY.

THE FLAMINGO

GOOD POINTS CAN BE USED FOR REACHING OUT-OF-THE-WAY PLACES. E.G. REMOVING LEAVES FROM GUTTERS, WEEDING THE BACKS OF FLOWER-BEDS, OPENING HIGH WINDOWS ETC.

BAD POINTS ALWAYS COME IN FLOCKS. SOMETIMES THEIR LEGS AND NECKS GET TANGLED AND IT TAKES HOURS TO SEPARATE THEM.

SURVIVE ... FLAMINGOES BY BUYING THE FOLDING TYPE OTHERWISE IT'S A NIGHTMARE TRYING TO GET THEM INTO THE CAR, IF YOU'RE GOING TO THE VET, FOR INSTANCE.

EXCELLENT FOR TRIMMING TALL HEDGES

FOLDING FLAMINGO

THE SOUTH AMERICAN BLACK-KNEED SCREAMER

GOOD POINTS
YOU'LL BE THE <u>ONLY</u> PROUD OWNER OF THIS BIRD IN THE COUNTRY.

BAD POINTS
SCREAMS.

SURVIVE
... THE BLACK-KNEED SCREAMER BY DROWNING OUT ITS SCREAMS WITH LOUD ROCK MUSIC OR TAKE IT TO SPORTING EVENTS AND LET IT SCREAM ITSELF HOARSE.

Creepy crawlies make fascinating pets. Children will easily survive creepy-crawlies but adults won't survive them at all.

If you're going to keep creepy-crawlies, remember these four golden rules:

On the next few pages you'll find a list of animals from our TOP FOUR most popular and unusual pets.

LARGE PETS →

1 GIANT CLAM

HUMOURLESS. FORGETFUL. APT TO SHAKE YOU BY THE HAND AND FORGET TO LET GO.

MEDIUM PETS →

1 WOLVES

YOU DON'T GET ONE WOLF — THEY ONLY COME IN SIX-PACKS OR TWELVE-PACKS.

SMALL PETS →

1 LIMPETS

FAIRLY TROUBLE-FREE BUT NOT ADVISABLE IF YOU WANT AN ENERGETIC PET.

There are also some points to look out
for if you want to survive these pets.

2 RHINO

CAN BE TETCHY.
A BIT SHORT-SIGHTED,
APT TO BUMP INTO
THINGS. HORNS BAD
NEWS FOR CURTAINS
AND UPHOLSTERY.

2 PORCUPINE

ALWAYS RATTLING
THEIR QUILLS WHICH
MAY CAUSE T.V.
INTERFERENCE.
DIFFICULT TO
WASH.

2 GOPHERS

WILL MAKE A
TERRIBLE MESS
OF YOUR LAWN
WHEN THEY START
THEIR HOUSE-
BUILDING
PROGRAMME

BEAR.

REALLY ONLY HALF A PET BECAUSE IT WILL HIBERNATE FOR ABOUT HALF THE YEAR. TRY A STAND-IN RENTED PET, LIKE A WARTHOG, FOR SIX MONTHS.

CROCODILE

NEEDS TO SHARE YOUR BATH. ALSO NEEDS TO HAVE ITS MANY TEETH ATTENDED TO REGULARLY. CHECK WITH YOUR DENTIST FIRST.

TERMITES

BUSY, CLEAN AND WELL-ORGANIZED. THEY'LL MAKE A TERRIBLE MESS OF YOUR LAWN WHEN THEY START THEIR HOUSE-BUILDING PROGRAMME.

GIANT CONDOR

LIKES TO FLY REALLY HIGH. MAKE SURE YOU'VE GOT A VERY, VERY LONG LEAD. LIKES ITS FOOD TO BE OLD AND SMELLY.

CHIMPANZEE

TOO CLEVER BY HALF BUT IF YOU DON'T MIND SHARING YOUR COMPUTER GAMES AND DRAWING MATERIALS, THEN A CHIMPANZEE IS WORTH CONSIDERING.

VAMPIRE BAT

TENDS TO TERRIFY FRIENDS AND RELATIVES OF A NERVOUS DISPOSITION. YOU HAVE TO STAY UP AT NIGHT TO ENJOY THIS PET.

Finally, do you really want a pet? It's a known fact that, if you keep a pet for a very long time, you will grow to look like your pet. You will see below some pets and some owners who have been together for a long time. Can you match them up? Remember, if you've had a dog for years and years, you may find people patting you on the head and asking your dog what the name of his pet is.

CLASSIFIED ADS

RHINO PROTECTORS

WOOLLEN HORN COVERS TO SAVE YOUR FURNITURE. AVAILABLE IN SIX COLOURWAYS.

Snake Coilers

KEEP YOUR SNAKE HAPPY WITH A SNAKE PERCH. EASILY ATTACHED TO WALL OR CEILING. SINGLE, DOUBLE OR MULTI-BRANCH STYLE.

SEND A S.A.E. FOR OUR LATEST CATALOGUE OF BIRD NESTS. TREAT YOUR BIRD TO A COMFY RESTING PLACE!

FLAMINGO DELUXE

WHEELED STORK

FOLDING OSTRICH IN TRAVEL CASE

ANIMALS JUST LOVE A DUST BATH SO LET THEM TRY A **DUSTO** DUST BATH

4 DIFFERENT SENSATIONS FOR THEM TO EXPERIENCE...

- SAHARA SERENADE
- DESERT DREAMS
- PERFUMED PRAIRIE
- WATERHOLE WALLOW

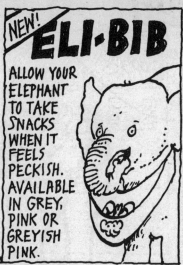

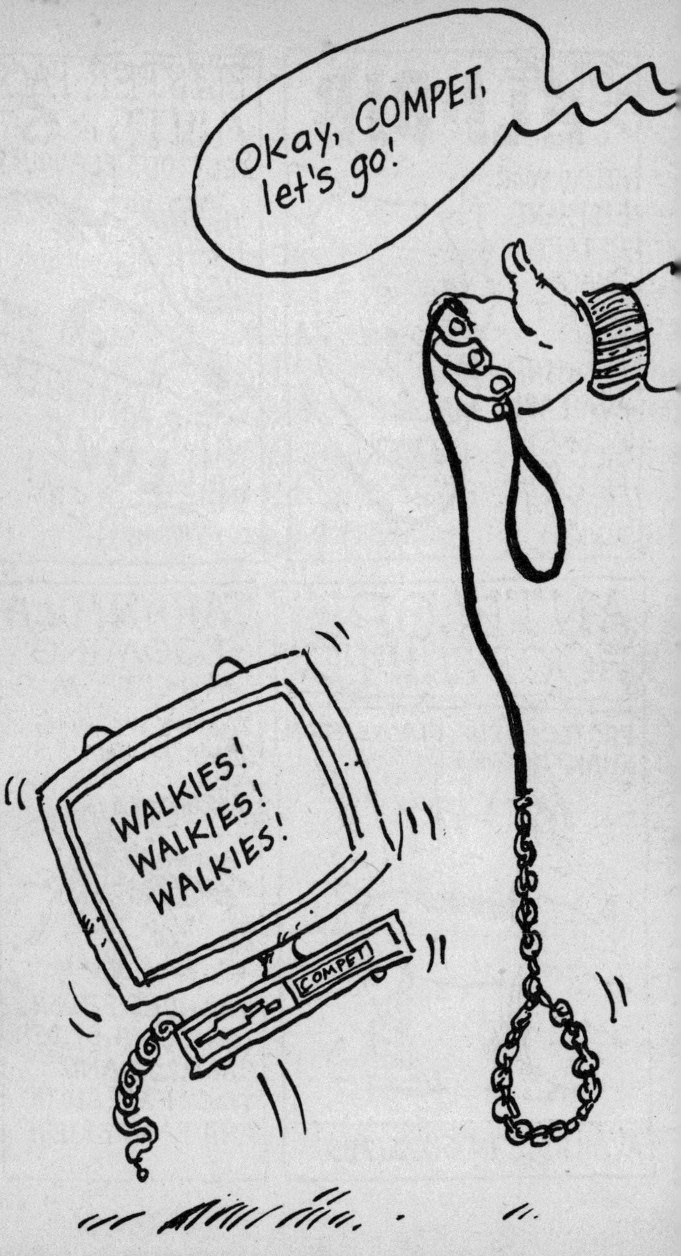
Okay, COMPET, let's go!
WALKIES! WALKIES! WALKIES!
COMPET